ICHE OTONTI

Happiness Health & Wellbeing Hacks

Simple Ways to Lift Your Mood & Energy to Create a Happier & Healthier Life

Copyright © 2022 by Iche Otonti

All rights reserved. No part of this publication may be reproduced, stored or transmitted in any form or by any means, electronic, mechanical, photocopying, recording, scanning, or otherwise without written permission from the publisher. It is illegal to copy this book, post it to a website, or distribute it by any other means without permission.

Iche Otonti asserts the moral right to be identified as the author of this work.

Iche Otonti has no responsibility for the persistence or accuracy of URLs for external or third-party Internet Websites referred to in this publication and does not guarantee that any content on such Websites is, or will remain, accurate or appropriate.

Designations used by companies to distinguish their products are often claimed as trademarks. All brand names and product names used in this book and on its cover are trade names, service marks, trademarks and registered trademarks of their respective owners. The publishers and the book are not associated with any product or vendor mentioned in this book. None of the companies referenced within the book have endorsed the book.

First edition

*This book was professionally typeset on Reedsy.
Find out more at reedsy.com*

Contents

1	Introduction	1
2	The Mind-Body-Spirit Connection	3
3	The Relationship Between Your Happiness, Health & Wellbeing...	8
4	The Mind-Body Feedback Loop	16
5	How to Create Gradual and Long Lasting Changes in Your Life	21
6	8 Simple Hacks for Your Mind	27
7	8 Simple Hacks for Your Body	37
8	8 Simple Hacks For Your Spirit	47
9	What Next?	54
10	Resources	57

1

Introduction

This is a self-help book that will give you some quick and easy steps to make changes in your life in a short period of time. It is not a quick fix book though, it is a book that requires you to make short term changes in a persistent, intentional manner and make them into habits that become long term changes in your life.

The book starts off getting you to have a better understanding of yourself and how some of your existing patterns of behaviour, attitudes and values have been formed and how they are the things that have a huge influence in creating the state of your emotions, health and wellbeing.

You are a complex being with many parts that are all interconnected to create the whole and sometimes we are unaware of this, or have lost sight of it along the way. Mind-Body-Spirit all work together.

You will begin to understand that you can do things that can change some of these underlying states of being that powerfully create how you behave and how your body responds to the environment around you in ways that may or may not be beneficial to you.

This book gives you simple things to do to make changes in your Mind, Body and Spirit and do so in small steps that build up to eventually make profound changes in your happiness, health and overall wellbeing.

If you have serious mental health or medical issues that severely affect you, then please seek help from a qualified expert who may be able to help you address these. This book can then be used as and when it is appropriate for you to do so.

In the past I suffered with a feeling of helplessness and depression and felt I was trapped in a never-ending hamster wheel of life. By learning about myself and how I was creating this life and then learning techniques to take control of my life I have come to a place where I am happier, healthier and have a feeling of peace I never felt before in my life.

There are many self-help books on this subject matter, but I try to give you a deeper understanding of what some of the changes can do for you and how some of the things I am advocating make a difference, not just in one area, but across the whole of your complex systems that all work together.

My hope is that you will find this book a quick way to kick-start changes in your life that in the process make you realise that you are a powerful being who has control over yourself and your life. I hope you will start on a journey of self-discovery and become happier, healthier and more content with your life.

2

The Mind-Body-Spirit Connection

What Does The Mind-Body-Spirit Connection Mean?

You as a human being are a complex interconnected sum of many parts that make up who you are, how you feel emotionally and physically and how you feel energetically.

Traditional thinking led us to believe that our body is a specific well defined entity that can go out of balance and develop diseases or illnesses which can then be treated with medication or physical therapy to return it to its state of balance and wellness.

Even the body was seen as a collection of specific organs and systems, and we have medical professionals that are experts in each of these specific systems or in specific diseases. So for example if you have a problem with your heart, you see a cardiologist, if you have a skin condition you see a dermatologist, if you have a problem with your brain structure, you see a neurologist and if you have a problem with your sinuses you see an ear nose and throat specialist and so on.

The mind was seen as a separate thing which could also go out of balance and develop neuroses and mental illness and we have a separate set of specialists - psychiatrists, psychologists, and psychotherapists to name a few.

It is interesting to note that neurologists who deal with the brain may be able to diagnose a physical cause e.g., a brain tumour, which can cause problems with the way our mind functions but by and large, the mind and the functioning of the mind was seen as a separate specialism altogether.

Where does spirit come into the equation and what exactly is meant by spirit in this context?

The spirit, again, was seen as a separate thing and was in the past regarded as under the auspices of religion and religious teachings e.g. Christianity, Islam, Buddhism, Hinduism, Judaism and many other religions.

We also had traditional religions and belief systems which were more aligned to the concept of the mind, body and spirit being connected, in a way that the more organised and rule-based prescriptive religions were not.

When I refer to Spirit, I am referring to that part of us that makes us feel connected to the world and universe outside ourselves. It is the part of ourselves that connects with others in meaningful relationships, that appreciates the beauty of nature, art, music and gives us a sense of peace and tranquillity.

Okay, you get all that but that still doesn't explain what the mind-body-spirit connection is so I will attempt to do so now.

I refer to the mind-body-spirit connection as the integrated whole where no one part is separate and unaffected by what happens in the other and all play a part in our happiness, health, and emotional wellbeing.

Ancient cultures and belief systems have always had that understanding but, with the advent of industrialised societies and advances in technology and more organised rule based religions coming into being there was a separation between all these parts of us with different people specialising in and claiming control over different aspects of society and indeed individual autonomy.

Why Is It Important To Understand The Mind-Body-Spirit Connection?

The concept of the mind-body-spirit connection is a return to what was already known in years gone by but fell out of favour in a bid to control society. The intrinsic loss of control over individual autonomy in favour of the societal rules and regulations then became taught in schools and fragmentation of the whole person has led to wide scale dissatisfaction with life and the need to numb ourselves with things to distract us from the pain.

We develop addictions and behaviours like excessive alcohol consumption, smoking, sex addiction, inordinate amounts of time spent on social media or watching tv, overeating and emotional eating to numb our pain and distract us from the dissatisfaction we feel about our lives.

Unfortunately, these behaviours rather than helping us, create more and more dissatisfaction, guilt, and self-criticism and sometimes even depression.

Developing the understanding that you create what is happening in your life, your mind, your body and your spirit will give you a sense of control and the ability to make change that can create a different way of being.

To take a simple example, what you eat affects your energy levels, your immune system and can also affect your mood and the state of your skin. This means that making changes in this one area can have an effect on many aspects of your life and because many of you have control over what you eat you can make these changes easily (unless there are specific circumstances that prevent this).

It is my hope that this book introduces you to the concepts of self-love and self-care and gives you some simple ways to connect with yourself in a deeper, more meaningful way that brings a greater sense of peace, joy and zest for life.

That said, it does not mean that society and our relationships with others are not important, but that the relationship we have with ourselves is important and is the foundation on which we can build relationships with others.

You have probably all heard the saying "Put on your own oxygen mask before attempting to help others with theirs". This is the same concept I am advocating, and many others do as well. Our relationship with ourselves is often neglected and we need to reconnect with ourselves and understand our whole being, mind-body-spirit to bring balance into our lives and then develop deeper connections with others.

What Has Shaped Your Unique Mind-Body-Spirit Connection

Every single person is a completely unique individual. Even identical twins brought up in the same family, though similar, will have differences in their likes & dislikes, attitudes, behaviour, bodies, brain chemistry etc.

Our childhood has a profound effect on shaping us and things like, our relationship with our parents and caregivers, our nutrition, the social and physical environment around us, our schooling, religious practices, the beliefs, attitudes, and rules of behaviour that we are taught and the experiences we go through. These shape our brains, our bodies and our psyche and affect our spirit.

As a young child, we do not have the critical and analytic thinking of an adult as our brains are still developing those abilities and in order to make sense of the world around us and the things that happen to us, we develop our own stories about what this all means about the world, about ourselves and about other people. This is an influencing factor on why siblings brought up in the same environment are different from each other and may have different beliefs and attitudes. These stories we make up are not real, but they can get built into our psyche and our way of viewing the world in adulthood.

This shaping of our unique being continues into adulthood and throughout our lives, but the foundation is laid down in infanthood, early childhood and adolescence.

3

The Relationship Between Your Happiness, Health & Wellbeing And Your Own Unique Mind-Body-Spirit Connection

How Our Childhood Developmental Experiences Help Shape Our Adult Attitudes & Behaviour And Can Create Unconscious Patterns In Our Mind And Our Body

Our childhood development has a profound impact on our beliefs, attitudes and behaviour, reactions to events and even our emotional makeup and siblings brought up in the same household will have many similarities whether they are twins or not. Even non-related children brought up together will have some similarities.

Below is a very simplified version of how we develop and how this sets up a blueprint for the way we think and behave.

Babies and very young children have sponge-like brains, without the critical thinking that adults have. This means the take in whatever they hear and see around them as the way the world is and what their place in it is. These imprints and inputs into babies' brains create chemical messengers - neurotransmitters, hormones, and other substances, which allow the messages they are receiving to be sent to other parts of their brains. When the consistent messages are sent over and over again e.g., when a baby is held and fed when it is hungry and cries, or has its nappy changed when it is wet and cries, the messages it receives are that when it cries it gets attention. They also learn that there is always someone there who looks after them. If the baby's caretaker is loving and caring towards it when it is being fed and changed, the feelings of safety and love that the baby feels create further chemicals in the brain that help the baby thrive.

Conversely, when a baby is fed and changed but shown no affection the chemical messengers sent to the brain are different and the baby may fail to thrive. It is reported that in an experiment alleged to have been carried out by King Frederick II in the 1940's, babies who were not talked to and were deprived of touch failed to thrive and subsequently all died.

Donald Hebb, a psychologist, is thought to have coined the phrase "Neurons that fire together, wire together." in 1949. This means that babies (and young children & adults) who are consistently fed the same messages over and over again will develop neural pathways in their brains forming a well-established memory which becomes part of their understanding of how the world / their caretakers are, and how they will be treated.

Not only can neurotransmitters be released by a baby as a result of the way they are treated, but also hormones notably oxytocin may also be released when the baby has a secure loving care giver who holds them and breastfeeds them. Oxytocin has beneficial effects on the physiology of the baby (as well as the mother). There are many other hormones and chemicals in the body that have an impact on us but that is beyond the scope of this book.

As you grow into a young child, adolescent and then an adult, the environment in which you grow and develop is constantly sending messages which cause changes in your brain and to your body. This is more so in a developing child as by adulthood we have formed our view of the world and tend to have more fixed attitudes and behaviour.

These attitudes and behaviour in adults can sometimes be completely unconscious because they have become memories that allow us to do things without having to think too much about them e.g., walking, speech and language, reacting to loud noises, reacting to other people's tones of voice and other social cues.

So far we have talked about neurotransmitters and hormones which are substances that affect our brains, and emotions as well as our bodies. Thus, we are already beginning to see the connection between our environment and early childhood experiences on the neural pathways that have developed and cause certain subconscious behaviours and have shaped many of our attitudes of how the world around us is and how we should behave.

Other inputs that affect us are things we eat and drink as the quality of these and the minerals, vitamins and other substances like sugars, fats, fibre, proteins, and micronutrients all play a part in the development of our brain and our bodies. The importance of proper nutrition starts even before birth and mother's whose diets are lacking certain essential nutrients may have babies born with low birth weight and other developmental problems.

In adults, nutrition plays a big role in our health, mood and wellbeing because our body and our brains need certain substances to perform optimally.

How Our Habits In Adulthood Create The Outcomes We See In Our Lives

So, we've had a brief introduction to how some of our beliefs, attitudes and behaviours are shaped in early childhood, but does this mean we are stuck in habitual ways of behaving?

No, we are not stuck and the brain is capable of changing and developing new habits and neural pathways if we choose to create the conditions for this to happen.

Neuroplasticity is the ability of the brain to change, adapt and grow new neural pathways. Remember the saying "Neurons that fire together wire together". If we make a conscious effort to create a new habit by doing something different over and over again, we can develop new neural pathways.

The opposite of neurons firing together wiring together is the "if you don't use it you lose it" This refers to the fact that we can forget how to do things if we stop doing them for a long time.

We can use this process to our advantage, and we can speed up this process of unwiring and breaking old habits, by becoming aware of them and interrupting the cycle each time they occur and by replacing them with something different. This is why some people are able to overcome addictions to alcohol, smoking, overeating etc. They break the cycle and replace it with something else.

Addictions can be very powerful as there can be a psychological element as well as a biochemical element to them (mind and body) and being able to overcome addictions show us that we have the power to change and rewire our behaviour and our body's chemistry.

If things as powerful as addictions can be overcome, it stands to reason that we can change other less powerful habits.

The problem, however, is that sometimes habits are so unconscious that we are not even aware of them and the impact they have on our lives. If we learn more about ourselves, we can begin to consciously make changes, should we choose to. The key thing here is "Choice". It takes effort and will to make changes, but you can do it if you make a choice to do so.

Some of the everyday habits we have developed as a society have a detrimental long term effect on our health and wellbeing and our spiritual health. Inputs to our mind-body-spirit cause outcomes to our health, wellbeing and happiness and these can be positive or negative

Certain inputs will lead to negative outcomes, and these include things like:

- Eating low nutritional value foods
- Drinking too much alcohol / drinks with high amounts of sugar artificial chemicals
- Lack of good quality sleep
- The constant barrage of negative events shown on news channels (bad news sells)
- Listening to music with negative or violent lyrics over and over again

- Spending vast amounts of time on social media with false or misleading information
- Spending time with people who have a negative outlook on life and leave us feeling drained and depleted

What's the big deal you may say, well, the effects of some of the above are things like:

- Low energy and vitality
- The body unable to repair itself
- Gaining weight
- Low immune function and susceptibility to illness and inflammation
- A sense of dissatisfaction with life as the "grass seems greener on the other side"
- A negative outlook of the world and of people

Some of the factors above may then lead to other consequences like lack of motivation, not feeling good about your body, increased fear and anxiety, and low mood. Are you beginning to understand the cause and effect of some of the things we do or input into our mind, body and spirit on our health, happiness and wellbeing,

The opposite is true of positive inputs you give to your mind, body, spirit that create positive outcomes that you enjoy having. Input more of the positive and you have more of the positive outcomes.

You can make a choice to change certain things that are causing unwanted / unintended outcomes and you can do this bit by bit. This book gives you tools that enable you to make changes in simple and incremental ways.

The Importance Of Human Connections

So far, we have been talking about you and your own being, but it is important to understand that human beings are social creatures and we do not live in isolation from others.

Our early relationships with our parents and caregivers played a big part in shaping us, but even if this was less than ideal, there are still things you can do to mitigate some of the early conditioning.

Our relationships are an important part of our lives and deep and meaningful relationships with others can enrich our lives and give our spirits a sense of belonging to something greater than just ourselves.

Some relationships can be enriching, whilst others can drain us and have negative effects on us.

We have choices to spend less time / no time at all with people who we realise have negative impacts on us and spend more time with those who enrich, motivate us and help us to grow.

You may sometimes be unable to completely cut off some of the negative relationships e.g. with our parents, family members, our employer or work colleagues etc., but strengthening your relationship with yourself and raising your energy and vibration can make it easier to spend time with these people without being so depleted and, may even cause a shift in such relationships.

The key thing to remember is you have choice, and you can control certain aspects of your life to make beneficial changes.

4

The Mind-Body Feedback Loop

Hormones & Neurotransmitters And Factors That Can Affect Them

I have talked earlier about the Mind-Body-Spirit being interconnected and this is particularly evident in the mind-body / brain-body responses to stress.

For simplicity, I will not go into all the biochemical and physiological processes but will give a simplified version of this below.

When our mind / brain senses danger it sends a signal to our body to prepare to deal with the danger and the body secretes various hormones like adrenaline and cortisol.

These hormones cause our heart to beat faster, our blood pressure to go up, our breathing to get faster. Extra oxygen is sent to the brain, and we become more alert and our senses like hearing and sight are heightened.

THE MIND-BODY FEEDBACK LOOP

What started in the mind, triggered changes in the body and these changes in the body then caused changes in the brain.

If the mind / brain then determines that the threat is over, it again sends messages to the body telling it the danger has passed and it can calm down.

Although the stress response is an automatic response not under our conscious control, how we are primed to respond to signals of danger can be held in our memory and as a result of high levels of anxiety or constant low grade stress in our lives can become maladaptive in that the stress response does not properly shut down and our bodies are constantly being triggered to release stress hormones.

The stress response is just one example of the way the mind and body work together causing powerful changes and how prolonged stress can have an impact on the production and balance of the hormones and neurotransmitters involved.

But are there things we can do consciously to create a positive mind-body feedback loop that gives us desirable outcomes?

Indeed, there are and one of these things is regular meditation. It has been shown that regular meditation can have positive effects on the brain and the body and provide outcomes like improved immune function, a reduction in anxiety, reduced cortisol levels, increased serotonin levels amongst other things. Thus, we can choose to do something that can have a direct effect on our health and wellbeing.

Other things that can create positive changes are our food choices. Certain foods will provide beneficial substances and raw material enable our brain to produce beneficial hormones and neurotransmitters e.g., serotonin that improves mood, whilst other foods can have a damaging effect on our bodies and our brains e.g., a diet high in sugar or processed foods and low in fresh fruit and vegetables.

So again, we are coming back to the realisation that we have the power to make choices that can enhance our overall happiness, health and wellbeing. Many of the hacks in this book give you the opportunity to do that.

Neural Pathways And Brain Plasticity

I have talked earlier of the concept of "neurons that fire together, wire together" and brain plasticity. Brain plasticity refers to the ability of the brain to adapt and create new neural pathways and unwire existing ones.

Brain plasticity is much greater in infants and young children, but adults still have this capacity but to a lesser degree so we can make use of this capability.

How then can you create change in your life making use of this capacity? You can consciously do so in 2 main ways:

- Unwire existing habitual neural pathways by interrupting behaviour and replacing it with something newFor example, if your habit is to come in from work and grab a beer or a sugary drink from the fridge, instead, when you get in and have the urge to go to the kitchen, go to another room and do something else that relaxes you in some way. You could sniff some essential oils, look at inspirational quotes, look at photographs of loved ones, play some music etc. The key is to replace it with something else that is enjoyable but beneficial to you. If you do this over and over again and make it your new habit, eventually the urge to go for a beer or sugary drink will no longer be your first impulse when you come through the door after work.

- Create new neural pathways by creating a new habit.Learn something new, wake up and do 15 minutes of meditation, wake up and do some stretches before you have your shower. Do things that you can easily fit into your existing lifestyle so that there is no excuse or reason why you cannot do it. Do it over and over again and you will develop a new habit which essentially is creating new neural pathways. When you make changes that are beneficial you will be releasing different hormones and neurotransmitters that will have a beneficial impact on your overall wellbeing.

Learning new things also primes your brain to expect changes and to look forward to new things and not just stay stuck in a never ending cycle of habits that you don't even think about but just do without realising the effects they are having on your mind-body-spirit

The Effects Of Trauma On Our Mind And Body

Trauma is a whole topic on its own that has only gained prominence in the last few years even though research and findings on this have been going on for years and years. There are many informative books that can give you a lot more information on this subject if it is of interest to you, and I have listed a few of these in the resources section at the end of this book.

In this book I will touch on it to give a fuller picture of the effect it can have on our mind-body-spirit and how it can keep us trapped in very powerful unconscious reactions and behaviours which some people may find very difficult to get out of without professional / expert help.

In his book - The Body Keeps the Score, Bessel van der Kolk states "We have learned that trauma is not just an event that took place sometime in the past; it is also the imprint left by that experience on mind, brain, and body. This imprint has ongoing consequences for how the human organism manages to survive in the present."

Developmental trauma occurs when infants and children grow up experiencing adverse experiences that wire their brains to cope with the experiences. These patterns of behaviour may not serve them in adulthood but are wired into their survival mechanisms in a way that makes it hard to release them without help.

Adults who experience extremely traumatic events may develop post-traumatic stress disorder (PTSD) which may also trap them in patterns of behaviour that have a negative impact on their lives.

In attempting to make changes in your life, if you are aware you seem to fall into one of the above categories, I urge you to first seek help from a qualified practitioner or expert to help you release some of the patterns of behaviour that have been programmed into your mind and body. These programmed reactions may prevent you from making the changes you desire as they are linked to your survival mechanisms and to most human beings the survival mechanism will, in most cases, take precedence over non-survival activities and patterns because the human beings are programmed for survival.

5

How to Create Gradual and Long Lasting Changes in Your Life

Create A Loving Relationship With Yourself

It is important for you to stop and reflect on how you treat yourself, understand what your habits are that are creating the outcomes in your life and above all, to value and love yourself.

Many people are their own harshest critics and do not give themselves the love , time and care they give to their partner, their family, their friends, their job and other significant people in their lives.

Choose to be kinder to yourself and give yourself permission to make changes that will benefit you and make you happier, healthier, and more vibrant.

When you catch yourself criticising yourself, notice it, don't make yourself wrong for doing it (we all do it to a greater or lesser extent), but replace that criticism with something more positive and loving about yourself. If you keep doing this over and over again you will start developing new neural pathways in your brain.

Don't get hung up about it but do it in a relaxed way making it a fun thing to see if you can notice how often you criticise yourself and learn to laugh at yourself for doing so.

Start appreciating and noticing positive things about yourself and acknowledge yourself for them. Appreciating and noticing positive things about yourself and others in your life will also be beneficial as it will begin to prime your brain to look for positive things rather than negative things about yourself and others.

These two practices will form an underlying basis for some of the hacks further on in this book. The aim is to have fun hacking our mind, body, and spirit to create more energy, more fun, more love, better health and a better feeling of peace and connection with yourself and others. It is never too late to make changes. Start where you are, start gradually and before long, you will begin to see the results of your efforts.

Learn Everything You Can About Yourself

Very few people really understand themselves, understand exactly what makes them tick, what makes their heart sing, why they do certain things, what motivates them to get up and go every day or what their core values are. We are not taught to do this and may even see" indulging in self-reflection" a waste of time.

The rate of marriage breakdowns is very high and is getting higher and higher, and I suspect it is because people are not taking the time to understand themselves and understand the person who they marry and just expect that things will work out. When you encounter a situation where your partner has a very different opinion on what should or shouldn't be done and this is very different from what you feel, it often creates real tension and feelings of incompatibility that seem insurmountable. Why is it that we should expect that if we love someone, they would have the same beliefs, attitudes and behaviour as us?

Getting back to the topic of learning about yourself, switch off from technology and social media and go for a walk, go to the seaside, do some gardening or anything else that will give you the peace and quiet to just reflect and think and discover more about yourself. We will go into this in more details further on in the book but learning about yourself is a powerful way to disconnect yourself from mindlessly just following patterns of behaviour and wondering why you feel trapped in a hamster wheel of sameness and boredom with your life.

Use Simple Hacks To Change Things Gradually

When learning something new like driving, riding a bicycle, learning to cook and so on, we learn gradually then add new elements till eventually we have mastered the skill and no longer have to think too deeply about it to do it. It has become a habit and we have built up neural pathways and muscle memories that enable us to remember how to carry out this new skill without too much effort.

This is the same way you should approach the hacks in this book. Try new things out and then add new elements as time goes on. Do things over and over again consciously until they become a habit and you don't have to think too much about them to do them.

Have fun with them and challenge yourself to see how much you can grow and change and be proud of what you are able to achieve.

My suggestion is to choose 2 or 3 hacks from different sections of the book and begin practising these consistently with an intent to make them a normal part of your everyday life. Once you have practised the new skills persistently and feel they are becoming easier and easier to do, then add new items to your daily practice.

You do not have to do them in the order they are listed or even do everything that is listed. Once you begin to know yourself better there may discover other things you would like to do that will make the positive changes you are seeking so by all means practice those.

The key is to make choices and to choose to be in control of the inputs to your mind, body, and spirit, rather than just let life happen to you. This feeling of being in control of my own life was what allowed me to move away from a life of chronic depression to one where I felt empowered and when I added new things and new skills and practises my life began to change in ways I could never have imagined. I have to keep being aware of what I am feeding myself and when I slip into behaviour that is not beneficial, I soon feel it and it is a choice then to change if I want to feel different.

It can be scary sometimes to make changes in your life and can be especially so if you carry a lot of unresolved trauma which keeps you locked into survival strategies. For this reason, if you feel yourself being constantly triggered and uncomfortable trying these changes, seek professional help or the opinion of someone who can have an objective discussion with you to help you understand why you have such difficulty with trying to make changes.

Be Patient With Yourself And Learn To Wait For Rewards

As with learning any new skill, it can take time and effort to learn and if you are also unwiring negative patterns of behaviour and attitudes, it will take will and time to make changes. Be patient, loving and kind with yourself and understand that you have chosen to make changes in your life that will be beneficial and with continued practice the new skills and behaviour will become more ingrained and you will notice changes.

Instant gratification is something we have become accustomed to in society, if we want something we go out and get it, we don't always appreciate and think about how long it took for a juicy apple to grow, or for a product to be made before we can use it. It is there, we want it, we buy it, we use it. Sometimes we even buy things before we have earned the money to pay for it.

Some things are worth waiting for and long term gains from these practices will greatly outweigh the short term discomforts from maybe not doing something which might have seemed like instant gratification but was actually damaging to you in the long term.

Learn to think of long term benefits and gains and take delight in seeing changes gradually come into your life.

Be Proactive And Persistent

You may encounter resistance from others who expect you to be and behave exactly as they have always known you to. Rather than bowing to this pressure, be proactive in taking control of your own life and if you are able or feel it necessary to, explain to others what it is you are trying to achieve. You may be surprised that they might even want to try some of the things themselves.

Be aware that you cannot force anyone else to change and essentially this is your journey of self-discovery and self-determined change and others are free to make their own choices.

Be persistent, remember long term gains over short term gratification.

Also remember "neurons that fire together wire together" and it takes constant and persistent effort to create these new neural pathways, but it is possible to do it. Think how proud you will feel when you realise you have created positive change in your own life purely through your own efforts and persistence.

Go for it! You can do it and have fun along the way.

6

8 Simple Hacks for Your Mind

1 Take Control Of Your Life

Don't let life happen to you. Make a conscious choice to take control of your life where you are able. We all have choices we can make, no matter what our circumstances are.

(Nelson Mandela was in prison for 27 years but he chose to do things to benefit himself and others, he exercised, he read books, he wrote, he educated himself and he chose to leave hatred and bitterness behind when he was finally freed from prison)

Choose to make the time to make changes in your life and think about what changes you would like to make. Be realistic but be bold and consider things that will have a positive impact on your lifelong term.

Making a choice will be a starting point to creating feelings of control and empowerment over your happiness, health and wellbeing and will prime your brain to expect some kind of action.

Write your choices down and keep a note of the progress you are making as you go along. Taking action shows you mean business and having something written down that you can refer to, will remind you what you are hoping to achieve.

If you want to take it a step further, visualise what changes you would like to see in your life and do this at least once every day.

2 Feed Your Mind With Positive Things And Reduce Negative Inputs

The things we listen to, say and watch every day create feelings and emotions in us and chemical messengers are released by our brain and our body in response to these.

TV news and news in general, tends to concentrate on the negative things happening in the world and so our responses could be to get sad, angry, fearful or indignant and if these are the constant input we are feeding to our brain, then our view of the world becomes negative, and this can affect our mood and our energy and create stress and anxiety.

Likewise, listening to music with violent or negative lyrics or watching violence and frightening movies or even playing video games where the aim is to hurt or kill others can also release stress hormones into our system. We are priming our minds and our bodies to be anxious or stressed or it can even evoke violent behaviour in some people if violence becomes normalised as it is in video games.

The reason why movies are rated and why some parents ban their children from playing certain video games is because with the developing brain it is hard to know what is real and what is not, and these things can create adverse reactions and unwanted neural pathways in the young brains.

The opposite side of the coin to this is that feeding our brains with positive reinforcing messages that fill us with hope and create peaceful feelings and chemicals in our body will have a much more beneficial effect on our health and wellbeing than negative messages will.

Examine what messages you are feeding your mind on a consistent basis. Are they helpful for creating health and wellbeing or are they detrimental to it.

Make a choice to reduce negative messages and even negative people as much as possible and make it a point to include positive and feelgood messages and inputs into your life to create more of the chemicals in your body that will be beneficial to you.

3 Learn New Things

Learn a new skill, a new language, do activities you have never done before to create excitement and a sense of achievement. Learning a new skill creates new neural pathways and if you are no longer doing something that was not so beneficial to you and are instead engaged in this new activity you are unwiring old pathways and creating new ones.

Choose things that you think you will enjoy, have always wanted to do or will be useful skills for you to have.

It is hard to be bored and depressed when you are actively doing something new that you enjoy. Keeping your brain actively engaged is also good for brain health and you may even find that your need for comfort foods decreases because you are getting feel-good hormones released into your mind and body,

This is particularly true of active sports as endorphins are released when we exercise, and these improve our mood.

4 Nourish Your Brain

Your brain needs proper nourishment to function optimally and although the brain is small compared to the size of the rest of our body, it uses about 20% of the energy needed by the body.

Eating essential fatty acids from food like avocado, olive oil, flax seed, oily fish, walnuts and almonds provide your brain with the basic nutrients required to keep the myelin sheath (the fatty tissue in our brain which protects our nerves and spinal cord and help our nerves function properly), healthy.

Diets high in fresh fruits and vegetables provide a wide variety of minerals, substances and micronutrients that are beneficial to the brain and the rest of the body. The mind / brain and the body are so closely interlinked with so many complementary functions that it is difficult to talk of brain health in isolation from the rest of the body.

However, it has been found that diets high in unsaturated fats and sugar can be damaging to optimal brain functioning and can play a part in worsening depression

If you are interested in finding out more about foods for optimal brain functioning, please see the link in the resources section which gives a review of 5 books on this subject. (Top 5 brain food books)

Don't forget about the importance of proper hydration for the health of your brain. 75% of the brain mass consists of water and research has shown that even mild dehydration can have an adverse effect on cognitive functions, memory, and psychomotor functioning.

5 Learn About Yourself

Creating a deep and meaningful relationship with yourself starts with understanding yourself better.

Choose to find out things like:

- How do I treat myself - am I super critical of myself, do I give myself love and care, do I feel I matter to myself or anyone else?
- What was I like as a baby and what was my early childhood like?
- What are the things I really like doing?
- What are the things that make my heart sing, fill me with inspiration and excitement, things that I would love to do?
- Who do I admire and why?
- What values do I have - what is important to me in life, in a partner, in friends?
- What are my relationships like with my partner, family, friends, employer (if relevant)? Do I feel good when I am with these people, or do I feel drained and depleted after being with them? Are there people I need to cut out of my life or spend less time with?
- What new skills would you like to learn?
- What would you do with your life if time and money did not limit you?
- What makes me angry, sad, inspires me, motivates me?

- How well do I communicate with others?
- Do other people know and understand me?
- Am I in control of my life or do I let life, others, circumstances decide my life for me?
- What things make me feel stressed and anxious and why. Is the anxiety and stress I feel justified by the circumstance or is it a learned behaviour from things that happened in my past?

These are just some of the examples of things you can get to understand better about yourself. It is your choice and you can choose to explore lots of other things about yourself as well.

Switch off, have some quiet time, go for a walk, go out in the garden, and just allow yourself to ponder and explore yourself and your life. When you do this, if there are things you discover that you would like to change, ask yourself why you would like to change them, how would that change benefit you, do you have what it takes to make the change. In all you do try to have fun and treat what you discover as exciting information that will empower you.

6 Challenge Yourself

Stretch yourself to go outside the box, try things you didn't think you were capable of, learn a new language, travel somewhere new. You could set yourself a target for a result or outcome you want to achieve, a time you want to better, doing something you were afraid to try.

The key is to give yourself a sense of achievement by going beyond what you thought was possible for you.

When you do this, you are teaching your brain and your body that you are more capable, and this primes you to try even more things. Keep changing the boundaries and stretching yourself further. Do things that are beneficial to you and others in the community and not criminal activities or excessively dangerous behaviour that could put you or others at risk.

7 Reduce and Re-frame Stress

The busy lives we lead rushing from one thing to another with lots of pressures and expectations of ourselves and from others can leave us feeling stressed and exhausted.

Where possible simplify your life. Do you do things simply because others do the same thing? Are there activities in your life that are of no real benefit to you or any others or really not important in the grand scheme of things?

Sometimes we are busy for the sake of being busy because we are avoiding facing something going on in our life. Are you doing this? Can you let go of some things?

Some people seem to be less affected by things than others and seem to be able to put a positive spin on things. If this, is you, well done. If it is not the case with you and you do get stressed and anxious a lot of the time, see if you can pinpoint any things in your past that may explain why you feel so stressed. It may even go back as far as your childhood and an example of this could be a person who was expected to achieve high marks or good results all the time and was criticised if they did not achieve the standard expected.

Do not beat yourself up if you feel stressed and anxious a lot of the time instead, try and understand why and if the level of stress is justified by the circumstance. If for example you work at night and have to walk through a high crime area, then a level of stress is justified.

But, if you get anxious if someone comes near you in a safe work environment, then the level of stress may not be justified if nothing has happened to you or anyone else in that work environment. In this kind of situation, rather than saying work stresses me out, I hate going to work, you may be able to reduce the feeling of stress by looking at the situation and re-framing it. You may for example tell yourself that the workplace is not in itself stressful but you feel anxious because you come into close proximity with others and you were attacked in the past by someone who came up behind you and grabbed you. You may then remind yourself that you know and trust the people at work and don't think they will attack you so you can feel safe at work. Visualise work being a safe place to be,

If your level of stress and anxiety is justified and is a direct result of things that are happening around you or to you, ask yourself if there is any change you can make or anything you can ask others to do or not do that would reduce the stress you are feeling. The thing is not to feel like a victim. Make a choice to do something. It could even be that when you find yourself feeling stressed you start doing some deep breathing and become aware of where in your body you are feeling the stress and choose to relax that area of your body.

If stress and anxiety is really a problem, seek help from occupational health at work, a counsellor, a person you trust to talk about your feelings or join a class that teaches you skills that make you feel empowered and more able to keep yourself safe from harm.

Don't do nothing as stress can silently create a range of health problems if you are constantly pumping out stress hormones all the time.

If you have a chance to remove yourself from the stress by changing jobs or staying away from the places or people that are triggering you then do so.

Arming yourself with tools that can help you consciously reduce your stress levels will be beneficial to you. Meditation, breathwork and exercises are all ways you can reduce the levels of stress in your system.

8 Seek Help From Others

If you find yourself overwhelmed, unable to cope with life or particular circumstances, try your very best to get help from others who are professionally qualified or experts in the problem you are trying to overcome.

I mentioned earlier on in the book that trauma and trauma responses can be very powerful in stopping us from making changes. If as a child, trying to improve yourself or doing something different got you in trouble or was dangerous for you, it will be very difficult for you to make some of the changes suggested in this book until you have got help to release the trauma.

For a better understanding of the way trauma can affect you see the books listed in the resources section by Bessel van der Kolk, Gabor Maté and Peter Levine.

Acknowledging that you need and deserve help is a very positive move to make and if you are able to take this step you should acknowledge yourself for doing so.

You may also just want help understanding a topic or hack in this book e.g., nutrition and there are many books and lots of information you can find if you want to explore this area further.

You are in control, and you make the choices that you think will be beneficial to you.

7

8 Simple Hacks for Your Body

1 Develop Healthy Food Habits

Nourishing yourself properly is one of the most powerful tools you have to make changes in your life. The nutrients in food nourish the brain, the body and can also affect our mood. The building blocks for the substances we need to create the hormones, neurotransmitters, and other chemicals the body needs to function optimally come from our food and drink.

If you have a health condition which requires you to eat a certain diet, please check anything new you intend to eat with your health-care provider to make sure it will not cause any adverse side effects with your condition or any medication you are taking. Be proactive, it is your body, so you need to look after it and give it things that are beneficial to your particular circumstances.

You can also use common foods to help various ailments. Hippocrates is thought to have made this famous quote "Let food be thy medicine, and let medicine be thy food."

There are lots of spices and herbs that have beneficial effects on your body and mind e.g. cinnamon, peppermint, coriander, turmeric, ginger, and garlic to name a few.

Proper nutrition is also important for building a healthy immune system.

However, our food and eating habits can be very difficult to change because there is often an emotional component to it as well as a social component. If your family all have an unhealthy diet and you come along wanting to eat completely different things that can lead to resistance from them and make it more difficult for you to make changes. If this is the case, arm yourself with knowledge and information and explain why you want to make changes and invite them to try some of the changes with you.

If needs be, you may have to prepare or buy the foods you want to eat. It is a choice you have to make yourself and a healthy diet can lead to a myriad of beneficial changes in your mind-body and spirit so it will be worth it to make sacrifices and overcome resistance.

Also, as we grow up, in some cases, parents show their love and affection through food especially presents of chocolates and sweets or birthday cakes on our birthday and this can lead us to associate different foods with comfort and love. Be aware of this and if this is happening with you, see how you can replace the comfort from food with something else that makes you feel better.

As a general rule, reduce the amount of processed food you eat, reduce the amount of sugar you consume, eat at least 5 portions of fruit and vegetables a day some of which should be raw.

Include things like oily fish, olive oil, avocado, walnuts, almonds, and other nuts along with things like flax seeds and chia seeds.

Remembering the notion that "neurons that fire together, wire together" develop new eating habits and unwire unhealthy habits. Where possible, avoid buying the foods you wish to avoid so that there is no temptation in the house should you have the urge to eat them.

If you eat because you are bored, when you find yourself getting bored write what you are feeling in your journal, find something of interest to do, drink some water, go into the garden, sniff some essential oils, or go out for a walk if this is possible. Do something that breaks that habit of reaching for food to fill an emotional feeling.

If you are drawn to comfort eating, again do something that distracts you from the urge or at least choose a healthier option like a piece of fruit instead of sugary, carbohydrate laden foods.

You will find that if you are eating a really healthy diet that nourishes your cells, some of your cravings may disappear as your body is getting what it needs and producing more beneficial substances that make you feel good.

There are so many useful books on nutrition and healthy eating and in the resources section you can find a link to the best sellers in nutrition on Amazon if you wish to get a book. I have also included links to some on-line sites where you can find further information. Arm yourself with knowledge. Remember you are taking control and making choices that benefit you.

2 Do Regular Exercises That You Enjoy

Exercise is another thing we often neglect when we lead busy lives, but exercise has many benefits for our mind-body-spirit and overall health and wellbeing.

The key to incorporating exercise into your daily routine is to find creative ways to fit it in. For example, if you take public transport to work, get off a stop earlier and walk where this is practical.

Take the stairs instead of the lift/elevator where possible. Even if this means you just take 1 or 2 flights and then take the elevator for the rest. As mentioned in the challenge yourself hack, challenge yourself to go further so maybe add another flight of stairs once you are fit enough.

Even doing 15 minutes of exercise first thing in the morning at home and then again in the evening will be better than no exercise and if you make this a habit, you will begin to see the benefits and can maybe also include 15 - 30 minutes during your lunch break - go for a walk, do some stretches, or even go for a quick jog if you have the means to shower and change at work.

Stretching, yoga, Qi gong, squats, wall presses are all things you can easily do at home for a few minutes in the morning and evening. There are also many other things so you explore and choose.

If you have time, have regular longer exercise sessions at home, at a gym, join an exercise class, team up with a friend to jog, join a team sport. Not only can doing exercise with others help you keep on track, it can also give you social contact and you meet likeminded people who also care about their health and wellbeing.

There are so many different ways to exercise so find a way that is fun, is within your capability and you can also challenge yourself to progress in. Build those neural pathways by creating a habit and release all those wonderful endorphins that make you feel good into your system.

3 Have Good Quality Sleep

Sleep is the time that our body is able to rest, repair and reset itself. It also allows our minds to process and work through things e.g. when we dream, so it is important to you that you get good quality sleep where you are able to go into the sleep phases where this repair and resetting can take place.

On average adults need approximately 7- 8 hours of sleep for optimum health. Children and adolescents require more sleep than this.

Try and create a regular time to unwind and get ready for sleep. Set an alarm to remind you it is time to start winding down.

If you need to get up to wee several times a night, try setting an alarm for at least 3 hours before bedtime and do not drink anything after this time. Rehydrate yourself when you wake up and drink adequate fluids earlier in the day.

You can find further information about the importance of sleep, and how to get a good night's sleep in the article Secrets of Sleep 2.0. The link to this can be found in the resources section at the end of the book.

4 Spend Time Marvelling At Nature

Being out in nature can have many benefits to your health and wellbeing and spiritual health - fresh air, connection to the wider universe, wonder at the beauty and diversity of the planet, being away from technology and electrical fields, immersed in the vibration from plants, sea, etc.

Taking the time to appreciate and marvel at the wonders of the natural world also gives your brain a boost of beneficial chemicals so when you do go out notice everything, wonder at it all and just enjoy the environment.

Being out in nature has been shown to reduce stress, lower blood pressure, and soothe and restore us. It helps us connect with the world and environment and realise that we are part of a much larger whole that all works together and needs to be looked after.

A great way of combining being out in nature and getting some exercise at the same time is hiking, gardening, walks in the forest, swimming at the seaside. Each of these have their own intrinsic benefits.

Gardening is a particularly good one because not only are you out in nature, but you are also nurturing and growing things and developing your ability to wait for long term gains rather than instant gratification. If you feed, water and care for your plants you will see them grow and develop. The same applies to you. Give yourself the right nutrition, hydration and environment and watch yourself blossom.

As always, if you are interested in more information on the healing power of nature find links in the resources section at the end of the book.

5 Have Meaningful Connections With Other People

Human beings are social animals and the need for social relationships is built into our make-up. However, not all relationships are beneficial to us. Some relationships can drain our energy, motivation and lower our moods.

Where possible try to spend less time with people that are not beneficial to your wellbeing and more time with people who make you feel good and raise your vibration.

Social media relationships can sometimes be shallow and false if people are just trying to show how wonderful their lives are when in fact this is not the case. Be aware that the grass is not always greener on the other side and people may be painting a false picture of what is actually going on in their lives.

A small circle of really close friends and family are much better than a large number of really shallow relationships with many people. Connecting with people on a deep level can cause beneficial chemicals e.g. oxytocin to be released into our bodies.

There are links in the resources section to further information on the benefits of relationships to our healths and some of the books shown there also give further information on this.

6 Reduce the Chemical and Toxic Overload To Your Body

The world we live in is full of toxic chemicals in the air we breathe, in the food we eat, in the substances we put on our bodies, in the makeup we use etc. Some of these chemicals have an adverse effect on our body's own production of hormones and chemical messengers and toxic overload is a big problem for some people.

Our livers, kidneys, skin all have to work harder to get rid of waste products and when we then layer all the toxic chemicals on top of that, they have to work even harder and can become less efficient at detoxifying.

Eating foods that help us detoxify e.g. lemons, coriander / cilantro, garlic, artichokes, beetroot, green tea, fresh fruits and vegetables help support our liver, kidneys and skin in their detoxification role.

Reducing the toxic overload however is a better way of dealing with this issue. Where possible, eat organic foods and use organic products free from artificial chemicals.

You can also make some of your own body products from natural ingredients ensuring you use organically grown ingredients.

Growing your own food is another great way of ensuring not only that you are eating organic produce but also really fresh food. Even if you don't have a garden, you can grow herbs and some green vegetables on a kitchen or other window sill.

Using a HEPA filter (high efficiency particulate air filter) is a great way of reducing toxic airborne substances from the air in your house.

Use cleaning products that contain a high percentage of natural ingredients and in some cases, you can make your own. Use steam cleaners to get rid of germs using just steam from pure water. You can also add antiseptic and cleansing essential oils to the mop head of the cleaners to leave a great smell in your home.

#7 Practice Breathwork

Deep breathing and specific practices where your regulate your breathing can be very beneficial in so many different ways:

- Better oxygen supply to your brain and your cells,
- Reducing feelings of stress by activating the parasympathetic nervous system which has a calming effect on your body
- Lowering your blood pressure
- Improve your energy
- Help you sleep better

Yoga, Qi-gong, Tai-chi which have been practised for hundreds or even thousands of years are built around using the breath and the benefits of regulating breathing have been known for all that time. However, more and more, breathwork practices are being developed and practised with corresponding benefits to health and wellbeing.

Breathwork can also activate our spiritual side and help us feel connected to the universe beyond ourselves.

As always, if you are interested in more information, you will find links in the resources section at the end of the book.

8 Pamper Yourself

Show yourself some love. Do something to show your body you care about it. Some suggestions are:

- Have a massage
- Have a reflexology treatment
- Have a soak in an epsom salts bath
- Have a pedicure
- Massage your hands and feet with calming or invigorating essential oils diluted in a carrier oil
- Have a lovely nourishing meal cooked for you
- Have a music or sound therapy session
- Take time out to go for a walk, go to the seaside, or do something you really enjoy.

Sending signals to your mind-body that you are important and giving yourself self-care can be very beneficial for your mental wellbeing as well as for your body. The list above is just a small section of things you can do. Remember you are in control, and you are beginning to understand what you like so make choices for yourself.

As always, if you are interested in more information about self-care and the benefits of it, you will find links in the resources section at the end of the book.

8

8 Simple Hacks For Your Spirit

 # 1 Do Daily Meditation

There are many different kinds of meditation - Guided meditation, meditation using a mantra, transcendental meditation, and mindfulness meditation to name a few. Some forms of exercise like Yoga, Qi-gong and Tai-chi also include some elements of meditation and breathwork within them.

Like breathwork, meditation has been practised for hundreds of years and lots of research has been carried out on the benefits.

Mainstream medicine has begun to recognise the benefits of meditation and it is sometimes recommended for certain conditions like anxiety, depression, high blood pressure and tension headaches to name a few.

Meditation enables you to relax your mind, focus your attention on something - a mantra, a guiding voice, a visual image, or your breathing.

Whatever the form of meditation that is practised, it becomes easier the more you practise - it becomes easier to go into the meditative state, you can go deeper into the meditation, your mind and brain waves slow down even more.

The effects of meditation are cumulative, and some research has found that long term meditation can actually change your brain. More details of this can be found by going to some of the links in the reference section.

Meditation is beneficial to spirit, mind, and body so it is one of those practices like nutrition that affects the whole of your being.

Explore the different forms of meditation available and choose one that you think suits you and start a habit of meditating daily even if it is just for 15 minutes to start off. You can incrementally increase the time as you get used to meditation.

The results come with persistent practice so keep at it.

2 Listen To Sounds And Music That Nourishes Your Soul

Sound is a vibration and vibrations impact our energy fields. Different vibrations have different effects on the body and the same is true of music with lyrics.

The sound of drumming has been shown to have a balancing effect on our brains and can help you feel calm and relaxed. Many ancient cultural rituals involved drumming for a reason.

Other sounds like Tibetan singing bowls, Gregorian chants and other chanting music can also slow down our brain waves and make us feel calm and more at ease.

Songs with positive and catchy lyrics like "Happy" by Pharrell William can actually make us feel good and raise our vibration and make us want to move to it.

Other songs with violent and negative lyrics or lyrics that demean others, can cause feelings of aggression and negative emotions.

Create your feel good playlist and listen to it when you need a boost or just listen to it because you feel like it.

Reduce or stop listening to songs with violent, negative or demeaning lyrics.

As always, if you are interested in more information on this topic, you will find links in the resources section at the end of the book.

3 Switch Off From Technology And Give Yourself Space To Just Be

Many people spend a lot of their time on their computers, both at home and at work, on their phones, tablets, on social media, playing games on said devices and watching TV.

This leaves very little time for our brains to unwind, reflect and relax.

Deliberately set aside time where you switch off from everything. Do some deep breathing, just sit and have a cup of tea or drink and just allow your mind to notice things around you and reflect on life.

Where possible go for a walk and get away from your 4 walls.

You can use the time to reflect, get to know yourself better and just switch off. Make this a regular habit and do it at least a few times a week if you can't do it daily.

4 Do Movement And Exercises That Calms Your Spirit

Certain movements and exercises like Qi-gong, Yoga and Tai-chi are often referred to as meditation as they involve some of the same elements - focused attention, rhythmic and regulated breathing, and visualisation.

These and other practices can soothe your spirit, soothe and centre your minds and make you feel more peaceful.

As this book is about you taking control of your life, do some investigation to find something that suits you and then practise it. You may already have incorporated something similar in your exercise section and it is fair to say there is overlap because it is all one interconnected mind-body-spirit system.

5 Connect With And Listen To Your Heart

Modern go, go go life keeps us in our minds a lot of the time and our feelings and instincts are often drowned out by the logical mind.

In meditation you are calming down the logical mind and this can allow you to connect more with your inner instincts and feelings - your heart.

Your heart contains a lot of wisdom and if you slow down and let answers come to you rather than try and force them with your mind, you may find yourself more in tune with what your heart really desires.

Stop and allow your heart to show you what would really make it sing and then follow some of that guidance.

You will find it more fulfilling to look within than to always do things that are expected of you or that you expect of yourself because of social conditioning.

The Heartmath Institute has done excellent research in this area.

As always, if you are interested in more information on this topic, you will find links in the resources section at the end of the book.

6 Show Kindness And Care To Others

A kind word, a kind deed makes you feel good and also makes the recipient feel good - a win-win situation.

When we are service to others it gives us deeper connection to others and opens up our spiritual side.

Do things for others not out of a sense of duty but just because you can and because you want to make others feel loved and cared for. Even small things can make a great difference to someone who is feeling lonely or down and you may be that spark that switches them to a happier place. What an awesome thing to be able to do.

Love and care for, and from, others make the world a kinder more pleasant place

7 Develop An Attitude Of Gratitude

Being grateful for things in your life and the things you see around you creates positive chemicals in your body and makes you feel connected to the universe, life and humanity and is good for your spiritual health.

Gratitude is a powerful emotion that can release feel good chemicals into our brains and bodies and regularly giving gratitude can retrain our brains to look for more things to be grateful for.

The practice of giving gratitude everyday lets the universe know you want more things to be grateful for.

Scientific studies have been carried out on gratitude which demonstrate that the positive changes are real and not just anecdotal.

As always, if you are interested in more information on this topic, you will find links in the resources section at the end of the book.

8 Forgive Yourself And Others

Forgiveness is about letting go of angry and hurt feelings and you don't actually have to talk to the person you are forgiving and in fact, may not be able to if they have passed away.

Holding on to anger, hurt and grudges has damaging effects on you and your health so letting them go is very healing and cathartic.

Forgiveness is not about saying what the person did was ok but is about choosing to let go of negative emotions you developed towards someone or a group of people. You are consciously choosing to remove and let go of these emotions.

You can choose what you want to do to forgive someone. Some ideas could be:

- You can write a letter and send it / not send it / burn it whilst visualising all the negative emotions being cleared
- You can perform any kind of ceremony that you choose where you symbolically let go of the negative feelings
- Ho'oponopono is a Hawaiian ritual for forgiveness that is a powerful way to forgive.
- You can speak face to face or on the telephone with the person you wish to forgive

The way you go about your forgiveness process is up to you but do make it a conscious process with some action steps that involve your body getting involved. This is more powerful than just thinking about it in your mind.

In the same way that you can forgive others, you can forgive yourself for actions you took in the past that were damaging to you. They happened and you can't turn the clock back, but you can choose to let go of the guilt and criticism and focus on more positive thoughts and feelings and choose to do things differently going forward.

9

What Next?

Putting It All Together To Create Balance & Harmony

I hope by now you will have understood that you can be in control of your life, your happiness, your health, and your wellbeing. Happiness, health, and wellbeing are outcomes that you can create and affect through your own actions.

I also hope that the mind-body-spirit connection is well understood and that the impact in one of these areas often has effects on the others. Thus, you will find that one hack can have beneficial outcomes to your whole being.

The cumulative effect of taking small steps and practising them over and over again creates new habits which help you rewire your brain and create a new you over time.

Creating balance and harmonious working across these 3 aspects of your overall being will lead to a happier, healthier and more content life.

Commit To Lasting Habits

Persevere and you will reap the long term benefits. Create new habits and they will become part of your life and will come naturally to you.

Explore and learn - become the master of your own destiny.

This book is just the tip of the iceberg for all the things you can learn and change in your life. You are in control of your life so you can choose other things that will be beneficial to you.

Exploring yourself, the world and things that are out there for you to enjoy and learning more about them, expands your world, keeps your brain healthy and active and will bring a sense of achievement and joy into your life.

Seek Help From An Expert

Sometimes we need help from others who know more about how to resolve an issue than we do.

I have realised that I carry a lot of stress within my body which comes from early childhood trauma and despite learning a lot about it myself it was not something I could resolve on my own and I am seeking help to free myself from the effects.

It is not a weakness to ask for help, it is a strength to be able to know yourself and know your limitations and then to choose to do something about it.

Never Give Up On Yourself

None of us is perfect so don't beat yourself up and have unrealistic and critical judgments about yourself.

Observe yourself, understand what has happened and refocus if you have let things slide. Just never give up. Keep going because you are worth it.

Reviews

I hope you have found this book useful and will put into practice some of the things you have learned to create positive changes in your life.

If you found it helpful, I would really appreciate it if you **leave a review of the book on Amazon.**

10

Resources

D. (2018). Frederick's Experiment. Digma.Com. Retrieved June 11, 2022, from https://digma.com/fredericks-experiment/

How Neurons That Wire Together Fire Together. (2021, December 23). Neurosciencenews. Retrieved June 11, 2022, from https://neurosciencenews.com/wire-fire-neurons-19835/

Moberg, K. U., & Prime, D. K. (2013, November). Oxytocin effects in mothers and infants during breastfeeding. Infant Journal. Retrieved June 11, 2022, from https://www.infantjournal.co.uk/journal_article.html?id=6635

Prado, E. L., & Dewey, K. G. (2014, April 1). Nutrition and brain development in early life. Nutrition Reviews. Retrieved June 11, 2022, from https://academic.oup.com/nutritionreviews/article/72/4/267/1859597

What is neuroplasticity? The brain's incredible ability to change itself.

(2021a, August 18). The Brain Charity. Retrieved June 11, 2022, from https://www.thebraincharity.org.uk/what-on-earth-is-neuroplasticity/

Firth, J., Gangwisch, J. E., Borsini, A., Wootton, R. E., & Mayer, E. A. (2020, June 29). Food and mood: how do diet and nutrition affect mental wellbeing? BMJ. Retrieved June 11, 2022, from https://www.bmj.com/content/369/bmj.m2382

Understanding the stress response. (2020, July 6). Harvard Health Publishing. Retrieved June 11, 2022, from https://www.health.harvard.edu/staying-healthy/understanding-the-stress-response

Xiong, G. L., & Doraiswamy, P. M. (2009, August 28). Does Meditation Enhance Cognition and Brain Plasticity? The New York Academy of Sciences. Retrieved June 11, 2022, from https://nyaspubs.onlinelibrary.wiley.com/doi/abs/10.1196/annals.1393.002

Davidson, R. J., Kabat-Zinn, J., Schumacher, J., Rosenkranz, M., Muller, D., Santorelli, S. F., Saki, F., Urbanowski, F., Harrington, A., Bonus, K., & Sheridan, J. F. (2003, July). Alterations in Brain and Immune Function Produced by Mindfulness Meditation. Psychosomatic Medicine. Retrieved June 11, 2022, from https://journals.lww.com/psychosomaticmedicine/Abstract/2003/07000/Alterations_in_Brain_and_Immune_Function_Produced.14.aspx

Xiong, G. L., & Doraiswamy, P. M. (2009, August 28). Does Meditation Enhance Cognition and Brain Plasticity? The New York Academy of Sciences. Retrieved June 11, 2022, from https://nyaspubs.onlinelibrary.wiley.com/doi/abs/10.1196/annals.1393.002

Wahl, D. R., Villinger, K., König, L. M., Ziesemer, K., Schupp, H. T.,

& Renner, B. (2017, December 6). Healthy food choices are happy food choices: Evidence from a real life sample using smartphone based assessments. National Library of Medicine. Retrieved June 11, 2022, from https://www.ncbi.nlm.nih.gov/pmc/articles/PMC5719018/

Charles, S. (n.d.). 5 Mental Benefits of Exercise. Walden University. Retrieved June 11, 2022, from https://www.waldenu.edu/online-bachelors-programs/bs-in-psychology/resource/five-mental-benefits-of-exercise

Wilson, J. (2018, December 19). Top five brain food books. Hometouch. Retrieved June 11, 2022, from https://myhometouch.com/articles/top-five-brain-food-books

Kempton, M. J., Ettinger, U., Foster, R., Williams, S. C. R., Calvert, G. A., Hampshire, A., Zelaya, F. O., O'Gorman, R. L., McMorris, T., Owen, A. M., & Smith, M. S. (2011, January). Dehydration affects brain structure and function in healthy adolescents. National Library of Medicine. Retrieved June 11, 2022, from https://pubmed.ncbi.nlm.nih.gov/20336685/

Adan, A. (2011, July 30). Cognitive Performance and Dehydration. Journal of the American College of Nutrition. Retrieved June 11, 2022, from https://www.tandfonline.com/doi/abs/10.1080/07315724.2012.10720011

Best Sellers in Nutrition. (n.d.). Amazon. Retrieved June 11, 2022, from https://www.amazon.com/Best-Sellers-Books-Nutrition/zgbs/books/282861

British Nutrition Foundation. (n.d.). British Nutrition Foundation. Retrieved June 11, 2022, from https://www.nutrition.org.uk/

Healthy eating. (n.d.). British Heart Foundation. Retrieved June 11, 2022, from https://www.bhf.org.uk/informationsupport/support/healthy-living/healthy-eating/

Healthy Eating Plate. (2011). Harvard T.H. Chan School of Public Health. Retrieved June 11, 2022, from https://www.hsph.harvard.edu/nutritionsource/healthy-eating-plate/

Secrets of Sleep 2.0. (n.d.). MedicAlert. Retrieved June 11, 2022, from https://www.medicalert.org.uk/news/2020/06/12/secrets-of-sleep-2

Strong relationships, strong health. (n.d.). BetterHealth. Retrieved June 11, 2022, from https://www.betterhealth.vic.gov.au/health/healthyliving/Strong-relationships-strong-health

The health benefits of strong relationships. (n.d.). Harvard Health Publishing. Retrieved June 11, 2022, from https://www.health.harvard.edu/staying-healthy/the-health-benefits-of-strong-relationships

Nature and mental health. (2021, November). Mind. Retrieved June 11, 2022, from https://www.mind.org.uk/information-support/tips-for-everyday-living/nature-and-mental-health/how-nature-benefits-mental-health/

Delagran, L. (n.d.). How Does Nature Impact Our Wellbeing? University of Minnesota. Retrieved June 11, 2022, from https://www.takingcharge.csh.umn.edu/how-does-nature-impact-our-wellbeing

Sifferlin, A. (2016, July 14). The Healing Power of Nature. Time. Retrieved June 11, 2022, from https://time.com/4405827/the-healing-power-of-nature/

Mahabir, N. (2018, January 12). From fight or flight to rest and digest: How to reset your nervous system with breath. CBC. Retrieved June 11, 2022, from https://www.cbc.ca/life/wellness/from-fight-or-flight-to-rest-and-digest-how-to-reset-your-nervous-system-with-the-breath-1.4485695

The Science Behind Breathwork. (n.d.). Backline. Retrieved June 11, 2022, from https://backline.care/science-breathwork/

Russo, M. A., Santarelli, D. M., & O'Rourke, D. (2017, December 13). The physiological effects of slow breathing in the healthy human. National Library of Medicine. Retrieved June 11, 2022, from https://www.ncbi.nlm.nih.gov/pmc/articles/PMC5709795/

Dolgin, R. (2021, May 28). Self-Care 101. Psycom. Retrieved June 11, 2022, from https://www.psycom.net/self-care-101

Scott, E. (2022, May 23). 5 Self-Care Practices for Every Area of Your Life. VeryWellMind. Retrieved June 11, 2022, from https://www.verywellmind.com/self-care-strategies-overall-stress-reduction-3144729

Meditation: A simple, fast way to reduce stress. (2022, April 29). Mayo Clinic. Retrieved June 11, 2022, from https://www.mayoclinic.org/tests-procedures/meditation/in-depth/meditation/art-20045858

Walton, A. G. (2015, February 9). 7 Ways Meditation Can Actually Change The Brain. Forbes. Retrieved June 11, 2022, from https://www.forbes.com/sites/alicegwalton/2015/02/09/7-ways-meditation-can-actually-change-the-brain/?sh=6ab1b8a01465

Alhawatmeh, H. N., Rababa, M., Alfaqih, M., Albataineh, R., Hweidi, I., & Awwad, A. A. (2022, January 13). The Benefits of Mindfulness Meditation on Trait Mindfulness, Perceived Stress, Cortisol, and C-Reactive Protein in Nursing Students: A Randomized Controlled Trial. National Library of Medicine. Retrieved June 11, 2022, from https://www.ncbi.nlm.nih.gov/pmc/articles/PMC8763207/

Pascoe, M. C., de Manincor, M., Tseberja, J., Hallgren, Baldwin, P. A., & Parker, A. G. (2021, May). Psychobiological mechanisms underlying the mood benefits of meditation. Science Direct. Retrieved June 11, 2022, from https://www.sciencedirect.com/science/article/pii/S2666497621000114

Allen, S. (2017, November 14). Five Ways Music Can Make You a Better Person. Greater Good. Retrieved June 11, 2022, from https://greatergood.berkeley.edu/article/item/five_ways_music_can_make_you_a_better_person

Ransom, T. F. (2021, July 31). A Case for Lyrics and How They Impact Our Emotions. Mappmagazine. Retrieved June 11, 2022, from https://www.mappmagazine.com/articles/a-case-for-lyrics-and-how-they-impact-our-emotions

Grace, J. L. (2021, January 25). Discover the benefits of sound healing for wellness and relaxation. Calmmoment. Retrieved June 11, 2022, from https://www.calmmoment.com/mindfulness/discover-the-benefits-of-sound-healing-for-wellness-and-relaxation/

Northrup, C. (2016, March 21). 10 Health Reasons to Start Drumming.

RESOURCES

Drnorthrup. Retrieved June 11, 2022, from https://www.drnorthrup.com/health-benefits-drumming/

Zuckerman, D. (n.d.). Violent Songs. Center4research. Retrieved June 11, 2022, from https://www.center4research.org/violent-songs/

Violent music lyrics increase aggressive thoughts and feelings, according to new study; Even humorous violent songs increase hostile feelings. (2003, May 5). Sciencedaily. Retrieved June 11, 2022, from https://www.sciencedaily.com/releases/2003/05/030505084039.htm

Riopel, L. (2019, September 25). 30 Meditation Exercises and Activities to Practice Today. PositivePsychology. Retrieved June 11, 2022, from https://positivepsychology.com/meditation-exercises-activities/#meditation

Goldsmith, B. (2015, March 16). How To Really Listen To Your Heart. PsychologyToday. Retrieved June 11, 2022, from https://www.psychologytoday.com/gb/blog/emotional-fitness/201503/how-really-listen-your-heart

Shapiro, E., & Shapiro, D. (2010, November 6). Listen Up! Why Being in Your Heart is Better Than In Your Head. Oprah. Retrieved June 11, 2022, from https://www.oprah.com/spirit/listen-to-your-heart-not-your-head/all

Exploring the Role of the Heart in Human Performance. (n.d.). Heartmath. Retrieved June 11, 2022, from https://www.heartmath.org/research/science-of-the-heart/

Morin, A. (2014, November 23). 7 Scientifically Proven Benefits Of

Gratitude That Will Motivate You To Give Thanks Year-Round. Forbes. Retrieved June 11, 2022, from https://www.forbes.com/sites/amymorin/2014/11/23/7-scientifically-proven-benefits-of-gratitude-that-will-motivate-you-to-give-thanks-year-round/?sh=2d8260fe183c

Brown, J., & Wong, J. (2017, June 6). How Gratitude Changes You and Your Brain. GreaterGood. Retrieved June 11, 2022, from https://greatergood.berkeley.edu/article/item/how_gratitude_changes_you_and_your_brain

van der Kolk, B. A. (2015). The Body Keeps the Score: Mind, Brain and Body in the Transformation of Trauma (1st ed.). Penguin.

Maté, G. (2019). When the Body Says No: The Cost of Hidden Stress (1st ed.). Vermilion.

Levine, P. A., & Frederick, A. (1997). Waking the Tiger: Healing Trauma (Illustrated edition ed.). North Atlantic Books.

Doidge, N. (2016). Brains Way Of Healing (1st ed.). Penguin Books Ltd.

Bruton-Seal, J., & Seal, M. (2022). Kitchen Medicine (1st ed.). Merlin Unwin Books.

Printed in Great Britain
by Amazon